I0881198

WORLD OF WORK

TRANSPORTATION

Exploring Career Pathways

Diane Lindsey Reeves

Created and produced by
Bright Futures Press, Cary, North Carolina
www.brightfuturespress.com

Published by
Cherry Lake Publishing, Ann Arbor, Michigan
www.cherrylakepublishing.com

Photo Credits: Cover, Beautyline; page 7,8, Angelo Giampiccolo; page 7, 10, benemale; page 7, 12, Dmitry Kalinovsky; page 7, 14, allstars; page 7, 16, goodluz; page 7, 18, Federico Rostagno; page 7, 20, Phovoir; page 7, 22, sevenMaps7; ZullU InFocus.

Library of Congress Cataloging-in-Publication Data

CIP data has been filed and is available at catalog.loc.gov.

Printed in the United States of America.

TABLE OF CONTENTS

HELLO WORLD OF WORK

This is you.

Right now, your job is to go to school and learn all you can.

This is the world of work.

It's where people earn a living, find purpose in their lives, and make the world a better place.

Sooner or later, you'll have to find your way from

HERE to THERE.

To get started, take all the jobs in the incredibly enormous world of work and organize them into an imaginary pile. It's a big pile, isn't it? It would be pretty tricky to find the perfect job for you among so many options.

No worries!

Some very smart career experts have made it easier to figure out. They sorted jobs and industries into groups by the types of skills and products they share. These groups are called career clusters. They provide pathways that will make it easier for you to find career options that match your interests.

- Architecture & Construction
- Arts & Communications
- Business & Administration
- Education & Training
- Finance
- Food & Natural Resources
- Government
- Health Sciences
- Hospitality & Tourism
- Human Services
- Information Technology
- Law & Public Safety
- Manufacturing
- Marketing
- Science, Technology, Engineering & Mathematics (STEM)
- Transportation

Good thing you are still a kid.

You have lots of time to explore ideas and imagine yourself doing all kinds of amazing things. The **World of Work** (WoW for short) series of books will help you get started.

TAKE A HIKE!

There are 16 career pathways waiting for you to explore. The only question is: Which one should you explore first?

Is **Transportation** a good path for you to start exploring career ideas? There is a lot to like about careers along this pathway. These professionals keep the world on the go with cars, trains, planes, and more. Now is an especially exciting time to work in transportation as experts rethink better ways to keep people moving in earth-friendly ways.

See if any of the following questions grab your interest.

WOULD YOU ENJOY taking pilot or sailing lessons, watching a NASA rocket launch, or helping out in the school carpool lane?

CAN YOU IMAGINE someday working at an airport, mass transit system, or shipping port?

ARE YOU CURIOUS ABOUT what air traffic controllers, flight attendants, logistics planners, surveyors, and traffic engineers do?

If so, it's time to take a hike! Keep reading to see what kinds of opportunities you can discover along the Transportation pathway.

But wait!

What if you don't think you'll like this pathway?

You have two choices.

You could keep reading, to find out more than you already know. You might be surprised to learn how many amazing careers you'll find along this path.

OR

Turn to page 27 to get ideas about other WoW pathways.

TRAIN ENGINEER

LOGISTICS MANAGER

AIR TRAFFIC CONTROLLER

WoW Up Close

Plan mass transit for millions of people. Direct traffic in the sky. Safely transport people and cargo by air, sea, rail, and roadway. Coordinate imports and exports to and from every corner of the world. These are just some of the important jobs that people who work along the Transportation pathway do.

AUTO MECHANIC

CUSTOMS AGENT

SEA CAPTAIN

TRANSPORTATION PLANNER

AIRLINE PILOT

AIRPLANE PILOT

Close your eyes and imagine sitting in the cockpit of a Boeing 747 jet. There are 392 passengers on board waiting to take off from LAX (that's the airport code for Los Angeles International Airport).

Your flight crew includes a copilot, two relief pilots, and a dozen flight attendants. Your destination? Hong Kong (or HKG, as its airport is known). Flight time is more than 14 hours, and there is only one way to get there. Fly across the Pacific Ocean! Ready for takeoff?

You are if you're an **airline pilot**. Pilots fly people and products to destinations near and far in airliners, military jets, cargo planes, and helicopters. They are in charge of aircraft that can costs hundreds of millions of dollars. Commercial airline pilots are responsible for the lives of passengers and crew. People everywhere depend on them to safely get them where they need to go. On time. With a minimum of bumps and bad weather. Without getting lost.

It's a big job that requires hundreds of hours of flight training. A college degree is required, and you'll need to pass written and flight tests to get licensed. Then it's up, up, and way for an exciting career in the sky!

Check It Out!

Find out how jet engines work at

- http://bit.ly/CathayPilot
- http://bit.ly/BeaPilot
- http://bit.ly/NATOPilot

Start Now!

- Use the Internet and library resources to make a timeline of the "history of flight."
- Fly around the world online with the Google Earth flight simulator at http://bit.ly/GoogleFly.
- See what you can figure out about how airplanes fly by making and comparing different types of paper airplanes. Get ideas at http://www.foldnfly.com.

AIR TRAFFIC CONTROLLER

There are no stop signs or red lights in the sky. No exit ramps or mile markers either. Yet millions of people fly into and out of 19,299 U.S. airports every day. How do all those airplanes move around the sky without bumping into each other? How do pilots know where to land and where to park their planes?

Air traffic controllers are a big reason why skies are safe to fly. Controllers direct traffic in the sky. They track, guide, and instruct airplanes (and their pilots) from the instant an airplane leaves a gate in one airport until it is safely parked at a gate at its destination.

The process is very organized, with different controllers responsible for very specific airspace. Some guide takeoff and landing, while others direct ground traffic moving from runways to ramps. Pilots must stay in constant contact with air traffic control throughout each flight.

Working with aircraft that move at more than 500 miles (805 kilometers) per hour leaves zero room for mistakes. That is why air traffic controllers must be highly skilled and well trained. The ability to handle stress and concentrate in a hectic environment are top skills needed for the job.

Check It Out!

Listen in on air traffic controllers during a flight from Los Angeles to Baltimore at

http://bit.ly/FAAFlight

Start Now!

- Visit a local airport and look for the air traffic control tower.
- Find out more about how air traffic control works at http://bit.ly/HowATCworks and http://playskyhigh.com.
- Try out some air traffic control **simulations** online at http://atc-sim.com.

AUTO MECHANIC

Anyone who has ever had a car break down (which is everyone who owns a car!) thanks their lucky stars when they find a good **auto mechanic**. Auto mechanics are trained professionals who keep cars running smoothly and safely.

Today's cars are high-tech, high-performance machines. Many of their systems are powered by computers. That means they are much more complicated to fix than those Model Ts that first rolled off Henry Ford's assembly line in 1908. Cars are also much more expensive than $825 like they were back then.

Auto mechanics must know their way around both computers and a toolbox. Many auto mechanics specialize in certain makes of cars—say Toyotas or General Motors. Other mechanics specialize in certain types of repairs, like bodywork for cars that have been in accidents or transmission or brake systems.

Taking auto shop classes in high school is a good place to start preparing for this job. You can also get training through community colleges and technical training centers. On-the-job learning and even apprenticeships can round out the experience you'd need to succeed as an auto mechanic.

Check It Out!

Get tips on basic auto repair at

- http://bit.ly/JumpBattery
- http://bit.ly/FixaFlat
- http://bit.ly/ChangeOil

Start Now!

- Volunteer to help your parent change the oil or a flat tire on your family's car.
- Find out more about how cars work at http://www.howacarworks.com.
- Put together a virtual toolbox by looking online for images and descriptions of "auto mechanic tools."

CUSTOMS AGENT

If you have ever visited another country on vacation, you couldn't leave home without your **passport**. You had to show your passport to officials at your destination to gain entry into their country.

When you returned to the United States, you had to show it to a **customs agent** at the airport to get back into the country. This is because, like all other nations, there are laws about who and what can come and go in the United States.

Customs agents are federal law enforcement officers who protect and secure U.S. borders. In addition to checking passports, that agent at the airport is responsible for enforcing hundreds of laws for 40 different government agencies!

Other types of customs agents work at shipping ports around the country. Every day they process some 68,000 truck, rail, and sea containers full of products. Other types of agents work at border crossings where they process vehicles coming in and out of the United States from Canada and Mexico. Still other agents patrol thousands of miles of land and coastal borders.

Needless to say, there is a lot going on when it comes to customs and border protection!

Check It Out!

Find out more about what customs agents do at

- http://bit.ly/BorderAgent
- http://bit.ly/CustomsAgent

Start Now!

- Look at the labels on your clothes and other household items, and make a list of all the imports from other countries that you find.
- For more information about how the U.S. customs service works, go online to http://bit.ly/HowCustServWorks.

LOGISTICS MANAGER

Logistics managers get products from the places where they are made to the warehouses where they are distributed to the stores where they are sold. It is their job to get the right products to the right place on time and at a good cost.

The job can get complicated, especially when you are importing products from other countries. Let's say a logistics manager has to get 25,000 pairs of blue jeans from China to a national chain of department stores in the United States. He or she would have to arrange for them to be shipped by cargo ship all the way across the Pacific Ocean from Shanghai to San Francisco. From there the jeans must be transported by trucks to regional warehouses in Denver, Dallas, Atlanta, and Newark. There are many details to consider and schedules to keep.

Don't forget the paperwork! There will be lots of it. Export forms for China. Import forms for the United States. People at the department store chain must be kept informed. Then there are the reports for the logistics manager's employer. It helps to be organized and to stay connected with technology.

It's all part of the **supply chain** of getting products from makers to buyers. And logistics managers are an important link.

Check It Out!

See **logistics** in action at

- http://bit.ly/SupplyChainGo
- http://bit.ly/FEDEXSupply

Start Now!

- Imagine that you own a big chocolate chip cookie factory. You are known for using the best chocolate chips in the world. Use the Internet and library resources to determine where to buy cacao (the main ingredient in the chocolate you make). Make a map showing how you will get the cacao from where it is grown to your factory. Be sure to include the different types of transportation you will need.

SEA CAPTAIN

For most people, the idea of "sailing the seven seas" is just a dream. For **sea captains**, it is a way of life. Sea captains are in charge of seagoing vessels used for both business and pleasure purposes. They guide ships traveling on rivers, oceans, and in and out of harbors. The vessels they command range from yachts, ferries, and commercial fishing boats to huge cruise ships, cargo ships, and naval battleships.

Even on smaller ships, the job is a big responsibility. There is no such thing as a cheap ship. They all cost lots of money, so protecting the ship from damage (and sinking!) is a priority. So is the safety of the passengers and crew. Speaking of the crew, the captain must lead them well. A successful voyage depends on everyone knowing and doing their jobs.

Of course, operating seaworthy vessels is not something that just anyone can do. Captains must have years of training and experience before they are qualified to take the helm.

One of the best ways to prepare to become a captain is to attend the U.S. Merchant Marine Academy or one of the state **maritime** academies. Only the best and the brightest are admitted, so keep those grades up if you hope to set sail on this career path.

Check It Out!

Find out more about what sea captains do at

- http://bit.ly/CargoCapt
- http://bit.ly/SeaCapt
- http://bit.ly/ShipCapt

Start Now!

- Ships use signal flags to communicate with other ships at sea. Use the Internet and library resources to explore "international maritime signal flags." Make a poster using these symbols to spell your name.

TRAIN ENGINEER

All aboard! It's 5:05 a.m. and time to get a train full of passengers to work. It will leave Boston shortly and make stops in Rhode Island, New York, New Jersey, Pennsylvania, Delaware, and Maryland. Its final destination is Union Station in Washington, D.C.

People will get on and off the train along the way. If all goes well, the train will arrive in DC by noon—just in time for lunch. This is the express train, and the **train engineer** will be making tracks!

The train engineer's job is to get the train and its precious cargo where it needs to go safely and smoothly. There is not a minute to spare, as people will be waiting at each station, expecting the train to arrive on time. Train engineers sit in the first car of the train in the engine room. There they control the speed and braking of the train. They also monitor weather conditions and keep tabs on nearby trains.

Some train engineers operate **subway** trains or local **commuter lines**. The engineers don't travel as far, and they make lots of stops. Others go back and forth along specific parts of long-distance routes. For instance, the train may be headed from Chicago to Denver, but a train engineer will drive for a few hours out and then switch trains and head back to his or her home station.

Check It Out!

Ride along with these train engineers at

- http://bit.ly/TrainEng1
- http://bit.ly/MetroTrainEng

Start Now!

- Use the Internet and library resources to find out more about America's first "transcontinental railroad."
- See how trains work at http://bit.ly/HowTrainsWork.
- Make a chart to compare the similarities and differences between traveling by train, plane, and ship.

TRANSPORTATION PLANNER

Transportation planners helps plan public transportation for cities. It is called mass transit because it involves BIG numbers of people, vehicles, and systems. Public transportation involves buses, subways, railroads, ferries, and bicycles. It can even involve walking trails and routes.

Take an **urban** area like New York City. It is home to one of the world's largest subway systems. There are 468 subway stations and 842 miles (1,355 km) of track. If you were to lay the track out end to end, it would go all the way from New York City to Chicago. Well over 5 million people use the subway every day. That is a big mass transit system! And that doesn't even include the millions of people who ride buses to and from work—or take the yellow taxis!

Someone has to plan all those schedules and assess where services are needed. They have to make sure vehicles and stations are taken care of. Transportation planners work on tasks like these. Safety and the environment are big concerns in transportation plans. There are also budgets to track and many regulations to follow.

It's a big job with many responsibilities. Sometimes, especially in bad weather, things don't always run smoothly. But on good days, transportation managers get a lot of satisfaction knowing you helped get so many people where they needed to go.

Check It Out!

Explore the New York City subway system at

- http://bit.ly/NYCSub1
- http://bit.ly/NYCSub2

Start Now!

- Take a survey of your classmates to find out how they get to school. Do they walk, take the bus, ride a bike, or come by carpool?
- Design the transit system of the future for your city. Include new ideas for moving people in ways that are convenient and easy on the environment.

Aerospace engineer • Air brake mechanic • Aircraft mechanic • Airframe and powerplant technician • **AIRLINE PILOT** • **AIR TRAFFIC CONTROLLER** • Assembly line worker • Auto body repair technician • Auto detailer • Auto engineer • Auto glass installer • **AUTO MECHANIC** • Auto paint technician • Avionics technician • Bicycle repair mechanic • Bridge operator • Bus driver • Bus mechanic • Cab driver • Cargo agent • Cargo inspector • Carman • Chauffeur • Chief safety and security officer • Conveyor tender • Crane operator • **CUSTOMS AGENT** • Deckhand • Delivery clerk •

WoW Big List

Take a look at some of the different kinds of jobs people do in the Transportation pathway. **WoW!**

Some of these job titles will be familiar to you. Others will be so unfamiliar that you will scratch your head and say "huh?"

Delivery driver • Diesel technician • Dinkey operator • Dispatcher • Distribution center manager • Electronics installer • Engine builder • Excavating/loading machine operator • Export coordinator • Field inspector • Field technician • First mate • Fleet manager • Flight attendant • Freight broker • Freight mover • Hand packer • Heavy equipment mechanic • Hoist and winch operator • Light rail operator

• Loadout supervisor • Logistics director • **LOGISTICS MANAGER** • Machine feeder • Manual materials mover • Material mover • Merchant marine • Motorboat service technician • Motorcycle mechanic • Navigator • Packager • Parts salesman • Railroad car welder • Recreational vehicle service technician • Recyclable material collector • Refuse collector • Sailor • **SEA CAPTAIN** • Signal maintenance technician • Signalman • Station agent • Supply chain analyst • Supply chain manager • Switchman • Taxi cab driver • Tire center supervisor • Tire technician • Towboat captain

Find a job title that makes you curious. Type the name of the job into your favorite Internet search engine and find out more about the people who have that job.

1. What do they do?
2. Where do they work?
3. How much training do they need to do this job?

• Tower operator • Track equipment operator • Track inspector • Track manager • Tractor operator • Traffic analyst • Traffic engineer • Traffic manager • Traffic signal technician • **TRAIN ENGINEER** • Trainmaster • Transit vehicle inspector • Transportation manager • **TRANSPORTATION PLANNER** • Truck driver • Truck mechanic • Tugboat engineer • Vehicle cleaner • Warehouse manager

TAKE YOUR PICK

	Put stars next to your 3 favorite career ideas	Put an X next to the career idea you like the least	Put a question mark next to the career idea you want to learn more about
Airline pilot			
Air traffic controller			
Auto mechanic			
Customs agent			
Logistics manager			
Sea captain			
Train engineer			
Transportation planner			

What do you like most about these careers?	What is it about this career that doesn't appeal to you?	What do you want to learn about this career? Where can you find answers?

Which Big Wow List ideas are you curious about?

Please do **NOT** write in this book if it doesn't belong to you. You can download a copy of this activity online at www.cherrylakepublishing.com/activities.

EXPLORE SOME MORE

The Transportation pathway is only one of 16 career pathways that hold exciting options for your future. Take a look at the other 15 to figure out where to start exploring next.

Architecture and Construction

WOULD YOU ENJOY making things with LEGOs™, building a treehouse or birdhouse, or designing the world's best skate park?

CAN YOU IMAGINE someday working at a construction site, a design firm, or a building company?

ARE YOU CURIOUS ABOUT what civil engineers, demolition technicians, heavy-equipment operators, landscape architects, or urban planners do?

Arts & Communications

WOULD YOU ENJOY drawing your own cartoons, using your smartphone to make a movie, or writing articles for the student newspaper?

CAN YOU IMAGINE someday working at a Hollywood movie studio, a publishing company, or a television news station?

ARE YOU CURIOUS ABOUT what actors, bloggers, graphic designers, museum curators, or writers do?

Business & Administration

WOULD YOU ENJOY playing Monopoly, being the boss of your favorite club or team, or starting your own business?

CAN YOU IMAGINE someday working at a big corporate headquarters, government agency, or international business center?

ARE YOU CURIOUS ABOUT what brand managers, chief executive officers, e-commerce analysts, entrepreneurs, or purchasing agents do?

Education & Training

WOULD YOU ENJOY babysitting, teaching your grandparents how to use a computer, or running a summer camp for neighbor kids in your backyard?

CAN YOU IMAGINE someday working at a college counseling center, corporate training center, or school?

ARE YOU CURIOUS ABOUT what animal trainers, coaches, college professors, guidance counselors, or principals do?

Finance

WOULD YOU ENJOY earning and saving money, being the class treasurer, or playing the stock market game?

CAN YOU IMAGINE someday working at an accounting firm, bank, or Wall Street stock exchange?

ARE YOU CURIOUS ABOUT what accountants, bankers, fraud investigators, property managers, or stockbrokers do?

Food & Natural Resources

WOULD YOU ENJOY exploring nature, growing your own garden, or setting up a recycling center at your school?

CAN YOU IMAGINE someday working at a national park, raising crops in a city farm, or studying food in a laboratory?

ARE YOU CURIOUS ABOUT what landscape architects, chefs, food scientists, environmental engineers, or forest rangers do?

Government

WOULD YOU ENJOY reading about U.S. presidents, running for student council, or helping a favorite candidate win an election?

CAN YOU IMAGINE someday working at a chamber of commerce, government agency, or law firm?

ARE YOU CURIOUS about what mayors, customs agents, federal special agents, intelligence analysts, or politicians do?

Health Sciences

WOULD YOU ENJOY nursing a sick pet back to health, dissecting animals in a science lab, or helping the school coach run a sports clinic?

CAN YOU IMAGINE someday working at a dental office, hospital, or veterinary clinic?

ARE YOU CURIOUS ABOUT what art therapists, doctors, dentists, pharmacists, and veterinarians do?

Hospitality & Tourism

WOULD YOU ENJOY traveling, sightseeing, or meeting people from other countries?

CAN YOU IMAGINE someday working at a convention center, resort, or travel agency?

ARE YOU CURIOUS ABOUT what convention planners, golf pros, tour guides, resort managers, or wedding planners do?

Human Services

WOULD YOU ENJOY showing a new kid around your school, organizing a neighborhood food drive, or being a peer mediator?

CAN YOU IMAGINE someday working at an elder care center, fitness center, or mental health center?

ARE YOU CURIOUS ABOUT what elder care center directors, hairstylists, personal trainers, psychologists, or religious leaders do?

Information Technology

WOULD YOU ENJOY creating your own video game, setting up a Web site, or building your own computer?

CAN YOU IMAGINE someday working at an information technology start-up company, software design firm, or research and development laboratory?

ARE YOU CURIOUS ABOUT what artificial intelligence scientists, big data analysts, computer forensic investigators, software engineers, or video game designers do?

Law & Public Safety

WOULD YOU ENJOY working on the school safety patrol, participating in a mock court trial at school, or coming up with a fire escape plan for your home?

CAN YOU IMAGINE someday working at a cyber security company, fire station, police department, or prison?

ARE YOU CURIOUS ABOUT what animal control officers, coroners, detectives, firefighters, or park rangers do?

Manufacturing

WOULD YOU ENJOY figuring out how things are made, competing in a robot-building contest, or putting model airplanes together?

CAN YOU IMAGINE someday working at a high-tech manufacturing plant, engineering firm, or global logistics company?

ARE YOU CURIOUS ABOUT what chemical engineers, industrial designers, supply chain managers, robotics technologists, or welders do?

Marketing

WOULD YOU ENJOY keeping up with the latest fashion trends, picking favorite TV commercials during Super Bowl games, or making posters for a favorite school club?

CAN YOU IMAGINE someday working at an advertising agency, corporate marketing department, or retail store?

ARE YOU CURIOUS ABOUT what creative directors, market researchers, media buyers, retail store managers, and social media consultants do?

Science, Technology, Engineering & Mathematics (STEM)

WOULD YOU ENJOY concocting experiments in a science lab, trying out the latest smartphone, or taking advanced math classes?

CAN YOU IMAGINE someday working in a science laboratory, engineering firm, or research and development center?

ARE YOU CURIOUS ABOUT what aeronautical engineers, ecologists, statisticians, oceanographers, or zoologists do?

MY WoW

I am here.

Name

Grade

School

Who I am.

Make a word collage! Use 5 adjectives to form a picture that describes who you are.

Where I'm going.

The next career pathway I want to explore is

____

Some things I need to learn first to succeed.

1 ______________________________

2 ______________________________

3 ______________________________

To get here.

Please do **NOT** write in this book if it doesn't belong to you. You can download a copy of this activity online at www.cherrylakepublishing.com/activities.

GLOSSARY

airline pilot
person who flies a commercial aircraft

air traffic controller
person who monitors and controls air traffic within a particular area

auto mechanic
person who repairs automobiles

border
the dividing line between two countries or regions

commuter
mode of transportation that carries passengers certain distances on a regular schedule

customs agent
person who works at an airport, border, or port to make sure that people are entering or leaving the country in a legal way

destination
the place that a person or vehicle is traveling to

export
related to products sent to another country in order to sell them there

imports
products brought into a place or country from somewhere else in order to sell them

logistics
the detailed coordination of a complex operation involving many people, facilities, or supplies

logistics manager
person who plans and coordinates the movement and storage of goods and services from origin to destination

maritime
having to do with the sea, ships, or navigation

passport
an official document that verifies you are a citizen of a certain country and allows you to cross international borders

sea captain
person who commands a ship

simulations
trial runs of real events

subway
an electric train or a system of trains that runs underground in a city

supply chain
the steps it takes to get a product or service to the customer

train engineer
person who operates a train

transportation
all the jobs involved in moving people and things from one place to another

transportation planner
person who coordinates plans, funds, and improvements for public road and transit systems

urban
having to do with living in a city

INDEX

*** Refers to the Web page sources**

About the Author

Diane Lindsey Reeves is the author of lots of children's books. She has written several original PEANUTS stories (published by Regnery Kids and Sourcebooks). She is especially curious about what people do and likes to write books that get kids thinking about all the cool things they can be when they grow up. She lives in Cary, North Carolina, and her favorite thing to do is play with her grandkids—Conrad, Evan, Reid, and Hollis Grace.